OUR DAILY BREAD
GUIDE TO EVERYDAY LIFE

PRAYING TO
CHANGE
LIVES

JODY BROLSMA

Our Daily Bread
Publishing™

For my daddy, Norm Wakefield,
who gave me a glimpse of
just how wild my heavenly Father is
about His children.

Thanks for always listening.
J. B.

Praying to Change Lives
© 2019 by Discovery House (Our Daily Bread Publishing)
All rights reserved.

Requests for permission to quote from this book should be directed to: Permissions Department, Our Daily Bread Publishing, PO Box 3566, Grand Rapids, MI 49501, or contact us by email at permissionsdept@odb.org.

Unless otherwise indicated, all Scripture quotations are taken from the *Holy Bible, New Living Translation*, copyright © 1996, 2004, 2015 by Tyndale House Foundation. Used by permission of Tyndale House Publishers, Inc., Carol Stream, Illinois 60188. All rights reserved.

Scripture quotations marked MSG are from *The Message*. Copyright © by Eugene H. Peterson 1993, 1994, 1995, 1996, 2000, 2001, 2002. Used by permission of Tyndale House Publishers, Inc.

Interior design by Michael J. Williams

Library of Congress Cataloging-in-Publication Data

Names: Brolsma, Jody, author.
Title: Praying to change lives / by Jody Brolsma.
Description: Grand Rapids, Michigan : Discovery House Publishers, [2019] | Series: Our Daily Bread guides to everyday faith | Includes bibliographical references and index.
Identifiers: LCCN 2018061298 | ISBN 9781627079303 (pbk. : alk. paper)
Subjects: LCSH: Prayer--Christianity.
Classification: LCC BV215 .B757 2019 | DDC 248.3/2--dc23
LC record available at https://lccn.loc.gov/2018061298

Printed in the United States of America
21 22 23 24 25 26 27 28 / 10 9 8 7 6 5 4 3

CONTENTS

THE WALL

When she opened the door, housewife Johanna Eck was unaware that her world was about to change forever. The Jewish man standing before her, Heinz Guttman, was at the end of his rope. After narrowly escaping arrest by the Nazis, Guttman had wandered the streets of Berlin. Friends shut their doors, fearing for their own lives. He lacked money, identification, food-ration cards . . . and hope. Recalling that Johanna's late husband had served with his father, Heinz knocked on her door.

And she opened it.

From that day until the end of the war, Johanna hid and provided for Heinz . . . then three others. She acquired additional food-ration cards from trusted friends. When air raids destroyed her home, she even secured safe housing for Heinz elsewhere. Johanna—a war widow and housewife—risked everything to stand with a friend and help. When asked why she went to such lengths, Johanna's response was simple: "The motives for my help? Nothing special in a particular case. In principle, what I think is this: If a fellow human being is in distress and I can help him, then it becomes my duty and responsibility."[1]

Johanna's story may seem like something from a movie, but she's not alone. Head to the United States Holocaust Memorial Museum and climb the stairs to the third floor. There you'll find an area called "Last Chapter" and a room whose walls bear row upon row of names. Names like Lucie Abel and daughter Lydie, Father Jean Adrien, Anton Dietz, and Anna Ehn. The names originate from twenty-one European and Eastern European countries. This is the Rescuer's Wall—a tribute to the thousands of regular people like Johanna who courageously stepped in to help during a dark and desperate time. The list includes schoolteachers, dry cleaners, actresses, doctors, and housewives. Rescue came from teenagers, and children as young as seven-year-old Helena Podgorska, who carried messages to Jews in the ghetto. These champions forged documents, hid families, and adopted children. Some helped one person. Some helped tens of thousands. They stood up for vulnerable neighbors and reached out to complete strangers. This list includes everyday people who gave hope, life, support, and a way out of a dire situation.[2]

Standing before the Rescuer's Wall can feel inspiring . . . and humbling. One can't help but ask, Would *I* have done something? Would *my* name be on this wall? What would *I* have to offer?

Today, you may not feel like you have much in common with such brave heroes. It's likely that no one is asking you to risk your life for a neighbor or hide a family in your basement. Although you may not witness historical atrocities in your community, hurting hearts *do* cry out to you.

"The doctor says it's cancer."

"Divorce seems like the only option at this point."

"Our finances are tapped out, and I still can't find a job."

"My daughter has run away."

"Mom has Alzheimer's. I'm not even sure where to begin finding help."

Those phone calls, Facebook posts, texts, or conversations over coffee can leave us feeling powerless. Like Johanna Eck, we open the door to a desperate soul seeking compassion . . . and we have to make a decision.

It's likely that your first response is "I'll be praying." But a whispered prayer seems so feeble in the face of hopelessness, doesn't it? Or is there more that maybe we're not seeing?

Listen, you may not be able to work miracles of healing. You might not be able to provide a loved one a new job, or change the heart of that unfaithful spouse, or help a lonely child make a new friend in a faraway place—but you *do* have access to the ear of a heavenly Father who can! Prayer has more power than we have yet imagined, and through lifting up the lives of loved ones, we come alongside them and carry them to the throne of Jesus. When praying, we can boldly become rescuers who offer hope in the face of desperation.

Do you believe it?

When you consider prayer, do you *really* believe its power is life-changing?

If you're honest, there are times you may not feel like your prayers have much clout. You may feel like you don't see fruit, or you wonder if God is even listening. You've likely prayed—with fervency and passion—only to hear silence. Or a gentle "no." Perhaps you doubt your prayer "skills" or secretly question whether there's some special prayer formula that might turn God's ear to your cries. While others seem like they could pray all day, you get distracted and begin making a grocery list after two minutes. Maybe you're unsure about prayer and fasting, kneeling in prayer, or even what people mean when they say, "God told me . . ." And, when the obstacle seems too big or heartbreaking or complicated or impossible . . . well, sometimes prayer can seem kind of small.

The apostle James encourages us: "The earnest prayer of a righteous person has great power and produces wonderful results" (James 5:16). *The Passion Translation* puts James's words in even more enthusiastic terms: "for tremendous power is released through the passionate, heartfelt prayer of a godly believer!"[3]

Need more encouragement?

> "LORD, help!" they cried in their trouble, and he saved them from their distress. He calmed the storm to a whisper and stilled the waves. (Psalm 107:28–29)

> Don't worry about anything; instead, pray about everything. Tell God what you need, and thank him for all he has done. Then you will experience God's peace, which exceeds anything we can understand. His peace will guard your hearts and minds as you live in Christ Jesus. (Philippians 4:6–7)

> I prayed to the LORD, and he answered me. He freed me from all my fears. (Psalm 34:4)

God's Word repeatedly reminds us that prayer has the power to bring miracles, peace, and freedom from fear. As you talk with God about the hurts and heartaches of friends and family, your heavenly Father doesn't misunderstand or ignore. God doesn't wait for perfect words or lengthy prose. God always, *always* hears. And God responds. Your words in God's ears are a formidable path to rescuing those in grim circumstances. Through prayer, you can courageously stand and support someone left weak or vulnerable by life's arrows.

For Johanna Eck, the step of faith began by simply opening a door and inviting someone in. Now her name is included with thousands of everyday people we proclaim as heroes.

What's stopping *you* from stepping out in faith?

Together, let's explore the marvelous things God can do when we open the door, invite someone in, and agree to help. We'll discover real-life ways to listen for God's direction in prayer. Through Scripture, we'll understand better how to ask without demanding, how to rejoice in grace when the miracle comes—and how to trust in faith when it doesn't.

Are you ready to feel excited to pray for others anywhere, everywhere, for anything—and find joy in the experience? Who knows? One day, you might just find *your* name written on heaven's wall of heroes.

CHAPTER 1

LIFE WITHOUT THUMBS

Before you settle in to read this chapter, I have a challenge for you. Ready?

First, hold out your hands, palms up, pinkies touching. Now lay your thumbs across your palms, as if you're showing someone the number 4. Got it? Keep this position. You no longer have the use of your thumbs as you attempt the following tasks:

- Turn the pages of this book to page 44.
- Open a door that has a doorknob.
- Pick up a coin from the floor.
- Tie your shoelaces.

How'd you do? (Oh, and congratulations! I've returned full power to your thumbs.)

Those little appendages are a pretty big part of our everyday lives, aren't they? Oftentimes we think of our relationship with God as the *heart* of our lives—it keeps us going and supplies life to every part of our spiritual body. But for a moment, think of your friendship with Jesus a bit like the use of your thumbs. It's a regular part of all that you do; it's something you can't imagine *not* having. You rely on that supportive relationship in each aspect of your day. Life feels strange or awkward without it. Knowing, loving, and talking with Jesus is right up there with breathing, seeing, and . . . well, using your thumbs!

If you've been a Christian for long, life without Jesus might be unimaginable. The love of our heavenly Father seasons life with purpose and joy. And the hope we have of eternity . . . we give *that* a resounding two thumbs up!

That's why one of our deepest aches is for our loved ones who don't yet know Jesus.

Perhaps you've been asking God to help someone you love to begin a friendship with Jesus. You've watched a friend struggle, and you know the comfort and reassurance Jesus could bring. A family member strives for wealth or prestige without understanding the pure joy Jesus offers. A coworker wrestles with addiction, but brushes off your attempts to share the hope of Christ. You've reached out to a loved one who flat-out rejects faith and says that religion is a lie. Your heart hurts for each of them because you know the peace and comfort *you* draw from your loving Savior. You see them labor to attempt life on their own, knowing it could be so different.

Jesus understands.

Jesus's heart ached for the lost. Even surrounded by critical Pharisees, clamoring crowds, and scoffing cynics, Jesus reached out in compassion.

> Jesus saw the huge crowd as he stepped from the boat, and he had compassion on them because they were like sheep without a shepherd. So he began teaching them many things. (Mark 6:34)

I once heard a wise children's pastor describe compassion to her Sunday school class as "your pain in my heart." Jesus felt the pains of the people in that crowd—their loneliness, doubts, rejection, anger, bitterness, sorrows—deeply within His heart.

Before soldiers came to arrest Him, Jesus spent time praying for His closest friends. He ended His conversation with God by lifting up those who would become His future followers.

I am praying not only for these disciples but also for all who will ever believe in me through their message. (John 17:20)

God's Son prayed for those who didn't yet believe . . . but who would. That's because God has a deep desire for people to embrace Him and experience His love.

More than anyone, God understands your desire for an unbelieving loved one to know Him. His passion for people burns so intensely that He looked outside the box to find the best person to grow His church. It didn't matter to God that the man for the job was one of the most ferocious *enemies* of the faith!

God had His eye on Saul, a religious leader who'd led the persecution of many Christians. God knew that Saul's energy and dynamic charisma—turned toward God—would speak in surprising and powerful ways to even the most determined doubter. Once God got Saul's attention by blinding him (a fantastic story we'll explore later in this chapter), look at the specific task God issued:

Yes, I am sending you to the Gentiles to open their eyes, so they may turn from darkness to light and from the power of Satan to God. (Acts 26:17–18)

God called Saul to open people's eyes. Incredible things happen when God opens our eyes to see His truth. It's likely that we've prayed for open hearts that are willing to receive God's love. But how often have we prayed for open *eyes*? What might happen if our loved ones could *see* something so undeniably from God that it transforms their hearts?

The prophet Elisha knew that sometimes seeing is believing! Second Kings 6 finds Elisha involved in something like divinely inspired espionage for the king of Israel. Back then, the King of Aram kept making battle plans against Israel . . . only to find the Israelite army had evacuated the area or avoided it completely when his army arrived!

Let's drop in and listen as the king calls his generals together. Imagine him giving each one a cold stare, then pointing an accusing finger around the room.

"Which of you is the traitor? Who has been informing the king of Israel of my plans?" (His terrified troops tremble a little, fervently shaking their heads.) "'It's not us, my lord the king,' one of the officers replied. 'Elisha, the prophet in Israel, tells the king of Israel even the words you speak in the privacy of your bedroom!'" (2 Kings 6:11–12).

Well, that made Elisha A–No. 1 on the king's Most Wanted List. (Maybe you'd have seen his picture on a poster in the marketplace.) After snooping around to find out where Elisha and his servant lived, the king sent an army to sneak in at night and surround the *entire* city.

Elisha's servant stepped outside the next morning and found himself eye-to-eye with a sea of troops, horses, and chariots. This looked bad. Really, *really* bad.

"'What will we do now?' he cried.

'Don't be afraid!' Elisha told him. 'For there are more on our side than on theirs!' Then Elisha prayed, 'O LORD, open his eyes and let him see!' The LORD opened the young man's eyes, and when he looked up, he saw that the hillside around Elisha was filled with horses and chariots of fire" (2 Kings 6:16–17).

Can you even *imagine*? What a game changer to realize that an angel army stood by, ready to fight for you! Disbelief and hopelessness evaporated when the servant saw with his own eyes the magnitude of God's power right in front of him.

Of course, praying for God to open the eyes of our loved ones doesn't necessarily mean we ask God to show them angels. You may ask God to display hope to someone who's struggling with hopelessness. A friend who sees the world as a hard, uncaring place may need to see tangible evidence of love and mercy. Unexplainable signs in nature move some people, while words and actions from children touch the hearts and open the eyes of others.

Prayerfully consider *what* your loved one most needs, then ask God to show him or her something specific. Pray, "Open his eyes that he might see . . ." Elisha knew that his servant needed courage, so he asked God to reveal the jaw-dropping army fighting for them. Visible signs of God's power or mercy can allow even unbelieving hearts to change.

That's because *prayer changes people.*

It changes the people we pray for, but it also changes *us.*

We pray for our loved ones because they're just that—ones we love. Their hurts are our hurts, and we yearn for them to experience the joy we know in Christ. But God's desire is for *everyone* to know Him. Chances are you've got someone in your life who doesn't know Jesus . . . but, in all honesty, it *hasn't* troubled your heart. When we see them fumble or struggle, maybe in our heart of hearts we think, "Well, they deserve it, after all . . ." or "Serves them right!"

What might happen if you prayed for God to open the eyes of someone you consider an adversary, such as a grouchy neighbor? An acid-tongued coworker? A cynical relative? You may feel God nudging you to pray for someone who's hurt or rejected you. That requires not only obedience to God but a heart change.

Remember Saul, the religious leader on a rampage against Christians? God didn't just grab Saul's attention. He used a guy named Ananias to help open Saul's eyes literally and spiritually. Imagine Ananias's reaction when God told him to find and pray with Saul.

"But Lord," exclaimed Ananias, "I've heard many people talk about the terrible things this man has done to the believers in Jerusalem! And he is authorized by the leading priests to arrest everyone who calls upon your name." (Acts 9:13–14)

We don't know if Ananias acted out of fear of the Lord, an obedient heart, or a newfound compassion for Saul. But Ananias obeyed and "something like scales" fell from Saul's eyes, allowing him to see everything in a whole new way. And the gospel had a new, dynamic champion who would go to the ends of the earth to share the news of Jesus's sacrificial love.

You and I can merely speculate about how Ananias felt as he prayed for someone who'd ruthlessly oppressed believers, but Gracia Burnham *knows*.

Gracia and her husband, Martin, served on mission teams in the Philippines for nearly seventeen years. A pilot, Martin flew supplies and mail to missionaries living in remote areas of the jungle. In 2001, as a celebration of their eighteenth wedding anniversary, Martin and Gracia took a much-needed vacation to a nearby resort. One night, a man burst into their room, taking them captive at gunpoint. That night, the terrorist group Abu Sayyaf took twenty hostages, including the Burnhams. For 376 days, Martin and Gracia survived as prisoners, enduring disease, brutal treatment, filthy living conditions, extreme hunger, and forced marches through unforgiving terrain.

Understandably, Gracia grew to hate her captors. In a fit of frustration and anger, she told Martin she wished she could see one, in particular, "burn in hell." Martin had a different perspective.

"Can you imagine witnessing the wrath of God poured out on a person?" he said to his wife. "Even thinking that should make you pray for Musab, not hate him."[1]

And so Gracia began to pray.

"You know what I found out? When you're praying for somebody, you can't hate them anymore. God changed my heart and gave me the grace to help someone instead of hate them. God is in the heart-changing business," reflects Gracia.

She recalls sixteen gun battles between the Philippine militia and Abu Sayyaf, in which the missionaries ducked their heads and feared for their lives. During the seventeenth battle, Martin was shot.

And he died.

Gracia was wounded, but rescued.

Years later, Gracia has continued to pray for her captors—and to reach out to them as well. She's made contact with several who are in prison. Four have started a relationship with Christ.[2]

Perhaps this is the transformation Jesus envisioned when He challenged people to flip common sense on its head, saying, "But I say, love your enemies! Pray for those who persecute you!" (Matthew 5:44). A heart change in Gracia eventually led to eternal change in at least four men who seemed beyond the reach of Jesus. Sometimes it's *our* eyes that need to be opened, simply to see people as Jesus sees them—as helpless, hopeless humanity in need of a Savior.

Consider this wise advice Paul shared with Timothy as Timothy began his leadership role in Ephesus:

> I urge you, first of all, to pray for all people. Ask God to help them; intercede on their behalf, and give thanks for them. . . . This is good and pleases God our Savior, who wants

everyone to be saved and to understand the truth. (1 Timothy 2:1, 3)

What a precious way to view *all* people—those we love and those we struggle to love. As you pray for God to open the eyes of your loved ones, ask God to open *your* eyes. Ask Him to change *your* heart toward people you may struggle to love.

Now, wiggle your thumbs and thank God for being such an integral part of every day. Next, fold your hands with your thumbs resting on top. Well, look at that! You're in a perfect position to pray for God to open someone's eyes and show them just how spectacularly He loves them.

PRAY TODAY

Close your eyes and thank God for all His gifts that He allows you to see—family members, nature, smiles, words of encouragement in the Bible. Now think of someone who *doesn't* see those things or who doesn't acknowledge them as gifts from God. Open your eyes and pray for that person, asking God to reveal himself and open that person's spiritual eyes to who He is and what He's done.

CHAPTER 2

UNFURL THE SAILS

The ship drifted in slow motion toward a collision course with disaster.

James gazed over the railing of the sailing vessel, frowning at the still, silent sea. Above him, the listless sails hung empty of the powerful breezes that *should* have powered the ship through the Dampier Strait and on to China. It'd bccn so long sincc thcy'd had wind, the crew began tying the sails back to keep them from flapping uselessly against the rigging. Without wind, the ship followed the mercy of the current . . . which swiftly pulled them headfirst toward dangerously shallow sunken reefs. The ship was a mere stone's throw from becoming wreckage.

The young man raised his eyes past the reefs to the Pelew Islands in the rapidly approaching distance. Natives lit fires and scurried around on the beach. Hadn't the captain's horn-book indicated these natives were cannibals? James gulped.

The captain approached and sighed. "Well, we have done everything that can be done. We can only await the result."

Something stirred in James's heart.

Had they really done *everything*?

"No, there's one thing we haven't done yet. Four of us on board are Christians. Let us each retire to his own cabin, and in agreed prayer ask the Lord to give us immediately a breeze."

With a shrug, the captain agreed. James and the other three went to their cabins to pray. He prayed briefly, feeling satisfied that God heard and acknowledged his request. With a renewed heart, James headed back up on deck where he found the first officer.

"Let down the corners of the mainsail," James said.

"What would be the use of that?" barked the ill-tempered crewman. Who was this landlubber—the only passenger on board, mind you—to tell *him* how to sail?

James explained that he and the other believers had been praying, and God would surely send a wind immediately. And with disaster just yards away, they should be prepared to act when God answered!

The salty seaman swore, giving James a condescending look. Yet he couldn't help glancing up at the topmost sail . . . and blinking. Was that a tremor? The sail stirred.

"I-it's just a cat's paw . . . a puff of wind," he stammered.

"Cat's paw or not, pray let down the mainsail and give us the benefit!"

Soon, the deck teemed with sailors busily unfurling canvas to catch the brisk breeze that grew with every second. Missionary James Hudson Taylor recalls, "In a few minutes we were ploughing our way at six or seven knots an hour through the water . . . and though the wind was sometimes unsteady, we did not altogether lose it until after passing the Pelew Islands."[1]

J. Hudson Taylor understood the impact of praying with a faith-filled heart and being ready to act when God answered.

Pause for a moment and answer this: In this account, do you relate more to James, or to the skeptical seaman? Why?

You may have a rock-solid faith because you've seen God do astonishing miracles. When you pray, it's with assurance and unshakable certainty. But many of us struggle with believing—*really* believing—that God can and will act on our requests. We ask hesitantly, or hold back our hope. "God, if you wouldn't mind . . ."

"Lord, if it's your will, maybe you could . . ."

"Jesus, I know you probably won't do this, but if it's not too much of a bother . . ."

Like the crewman, we've tied back our sense of anticipation and joy. We've packed away the possibility that God might do something amazing. We're afraid of looking silly or having a childlike sense of excitement that God is going to do something incredible. After all, we've been there when God said no. What if *this* is one of those times?

King David's outlook on prayer reflects a more tender, faith-filled attitude:

Listen to my voice in the morning, Lord.
Each morning I bring my requests to you and
wait expectantly. (Psalm 5:3)

There's a short scene in the Pixar animated movie *The Incredibles* in which a small boy watches Mr. Incredible (a superhero disguised as regular guy Bob Parr) coming home from a hard day at work. The boy, who'd earlier witnessed his somewhat-boring-and-seemingly-normal neighbor lift a car over his head, sits on his bike watching with wide eyes. A weary, and *un*incredible, Bob Parr pulls into the driveway and sees the boy.

"Well what are *you* waiting for?" Bob grumbles.

"I dunno." The boy shrugs. "Something amazing, I guess."[2]

I wonder what it would take for you and I to have that same sense of suspense and wonder at what *God* will do next; for us to be watching and waiting, wide-eyed. As J. Hudson Taylor experienced, praying with an unwavering, wholehearted hope puts us in a position to move forward when God opens a door.

Nehemiah writes about the impact of praying with confidence and living in a state of readiness. Finally freed from Babylonian captivity, the Jews joyously returned to Jerusalem. As the cupbearer to the Persian king, Nehemiah held a valuable position, so he didn't go. But he heard the not-so-great report from his brother, Hanani.

> Things are not going well for those who returned to the province of Judah. They are in great trouble and disgrace. The wall of Jerusalem has been torn down, and the gates have been destroyed by fire. (Nehemiah 1:3)

This situation left the already weakened Jews vulnerable to just about any enemy who might attack. An unprotected city equaled defenseless inhabitants. And God's people had already seen how ruthless and swift their enemies could be. Heartbroken for his people, Nehemiah wept, prayed, and fasted for several days. During this time, it's clear that he had a solution in mind—one that involved himself. He didn't just cry out to God, asking God to do something about it. Nehemiah formulated a plan of action during that time, and asked God to give him favor with the king to pull it off.

> Please grant me success today by making the king favorable to me. Put it into his heart to be kind to me. (Nehemiah 1:11)

Nehemiah stayed in this state of anticipation before God for *four months*! He prayed, hoped, and looked for opportunities to address the king about his kinsmen and countrymen. His sails stayed unfurled, ready to capture the first hint of a breeze. So when God cracked the door open, Nehemiah was prepared to stride through.

It happened on a regular day, when Nehemiah set the king's wine in front of him. Perhaps Nehemiah had been missing his family or pondering what might be happening in Jerusalem. Whatever he felt, something in Nehemiah's face looked different that day. The king noticed, and asked what was wrong. Here's how Nehemiah jumped in:

> Then I was terrified, but I replied, "Long live the king! How can I not be sad? For the city where my ancestors are buried is in ruins, and the gates have been destroyed by fire."
>
> The king asked, "Well, how can I help you?"
>
> With a prayer to the God of heaven, I replied, "If it please the king, and if you are pleased with me, your servant, send me to Judah to rebuild the city where my ancestors are buried." (Nehemiah 2:2–5)

Nehemiah didn't only pray with expectation, he positioned himself physically and spiritually to take action when God said "go."

As you lift up the burdens of your loved ones, are you prepared to set sail and take advantage of the breath that God sends? Certainly, there are times when God calls us to wait patiently for Him and allow Him to move. But what is *our* course of action when God *does* move? Friends, we need to be ready to jump from our knees to our feet! In Matthew 7:7–8, Jesus challenges us to "keep on asking, and you will receive what you ask for. Keep on seeking, and you will find. Keep on knocking, and the door will be opened to you. For everyone who asks, receives. Everyone who seeks, finds. And to everyone who knocks, the door will be opened."

Asking, seeking, and knocking are actions! What will you do when God *does* open the door? There's power when we turn our hearts *and* our feet toward Jesus in a spirit of confidence and expectancy.

Consider the men who brought their paralyzed friend to Jesus in Mark 2. If these men are anything like you, they'd have probably done everything they could for their friend—prayed for him, taken him to the synagogue, and asked religious leaders to bless him. But when they heard of this Galilean rabbi named Jesus, they knew *this* was the guy! *And* He'd come right here to their hometown! Wow!

Yet news of Jesus's teachings and miracles had spread to everyone, and the house where Jesus was staying became packed. Eager listeners wedged together like sardines, with a crowd blocking the door. So . . . how to get their friend an audience with Jesus? I'm not sure if *I* would have had the audacity to dig a hole in the ceiling, but apparently these men would do *anything* for their buddy. As a result, Jesus not only healed him, but forgave his sins as well. Four men believed that if *anyone* could help their friend, it was Jesus. Then they did whatever it took to bring their friend before the Teacher.

Are we ready to do the same?

As you bring your loved ones before Christ, open your heart with joyful anticipation. Prepare your feet to take action when God sends that first breath of breeze. And get ready to see surprising changes that will carry your faith to new adventures.

PRAY TODAY

Reflect on Jesus's words in Matthew 7:7–8 Write a prayer request—even a name or word—on a sticky note and put it on a door. Every time you use that door, pray and ask God to "open the door" with opportunity for you to spring into action about that request.

CHAPTER 3

NOT SO FAST . . .

Let's pause our prayer discoveries for a short time test. No, not a timed test like you took in elementary math class. A *time* test.

Set your phone timer for three minutes, press start, and then turn the phone over so you can't see the timer. Got it? Now, your goal is to pick up the phone only once—when the timer has *exactly* one minute remaining. (And no peeking at any other clocks!)

What should we talk about while you wait? How's your day going? Any plans for the weekend? How about this weather we've been having?

Once you've picked up the phone, go ahead and turn off the timer. How'd you do on your time test?

Did you peek too soon? Too late? Maybe you got it just right. If so, congratulations!

Let's reflect on the concept of time for just a minute . . . or five. It may be cliché but time really *does* fly when you're having fun. Not so much when things *aren't* fun. Have you ever taken a gym class that required you to hold a plank or do push-ups for one minute? That minute probably felt like fifteen! On the other hand, if you're having coffee with a treasured friend or savoring an ice cream sundae, a minute sails by in a flash.

It's no surprise that, when we're facing difficulty or pain, we want it over quickly. That's just human nature. But today more than ever we see waiting or enduring discomfort as an inconvenience. Ours is a "microwave" culture in which answers come at the speed of the internet and packages arrive in twenty-four hours. We're surrounded by fast food, instant messaging, and speed dating. We wait for nothing.

God doesn't quite work that way, does He?

For you, a thousand years are as a passing day, as brief as a few night hours. (Psalm 90:4)

But you must not forget this one thing, dear friends: A day is like a thousand years to

34

the Lord, and a thousand years is like a day. (2 Peter 3:8)

It's no wonder that we struggle when God says "wait." God doesn't view time, events, or history with our same limited viewpoint. And sometimes He asks us to wait and endure the discomfort longer than we'd like.

"I've been praying for a spouse for years. Will God answer before it's too late?"

"It's been a decade and my son is still distant from God and our family. It's heartbreaking to watch our relationship slip away."

"I've been out of work for six months. Why is God dragging His feet?"

Standing with a hurting friend, bringing a heartfelt prayer before God, waiting for—and understanding—His timing can be painful. We don't wait very well.

Neither did God's chosen people, the Israelites.

Exodus 32 finds the anxious Israelites awaiting Moses's return from Mount Sinai, where he's been meeting with God for about six weeks. In their eyes, Moses and God seemed MIA, and it was time to find a deity they could see and touch. They needed divine direction, and idols had always seemed to work for the Egyptians, right?

So the mob descended on second-in-command, Aaron.

> "Come on," they said, "make us some gods who can lead us. We don't know what happened to this fellow Moses, who brought us here from the land of Egypt." (Exodus 32:1)

Before you could shake the dust from your sandals, Aaron rounded up everyone's gold earrings and made a gold calf for them to worship. No waiting, no worry. And . . . no good! As a result, God nearly destroyed them, Aaron told an outrageous lie, Moses broke the original tablets containing God's commandments, and God sent a plague on all the people.

There are consequences when we don't wait for God's timing.

We're tempted to take matters into our own hands. We begin to doubt God's authority and goodness. We settle for second best. When we exchange God's masterful, perfect timing for our immediate desires, we're left with shabby—or even disastrous—results.

So why does God push the pause button on our prayer requests? Why does God ask us to wait when He knows it's so hard? Does God take pleasure in drawing out the suspense? Is it a heavenly power trip?

Let's explore what happened when one heartbroken woman had to wait on God's timing.

First Samuel 1 introduces us to Hannah. Year after year, she asked God for a child . . . but no child came. Her arms and her womb stayed empty. We can imagine Hannah's despair, as every month she got her hopes up, only to have them crash and shatter. To make matters worse, her husband, Elkanah, had a second wife named Peninnah who had many sons.

Apparently mean girls aren't just a modern phenomenon, because Peninnah ridiculed Hannah mercilessly. And husband Elkanah couldn't comprehend the depth of Hannah's longing. Seeing her tears, he offered well-meaning (but unhelpful) words: "Why be downhearted just because you have no children? You have me—isn't that better than having ten sons?" (1 Samuel 1:8). It's likely that Hannah felt isolated and alone in her grief. Perhaps that's why, during an annual trip to the Tabernacle for sacrifice and prayer, Hannah slipped away to pour out her heart to God . . . again.

"Hannah was in deep anguish, crying bitterly as she prayed to the LORD" (1 Samuel 1:10). *The Message* translation describes Hannah's state as "crushed in soul." Years of disappointment had brought Hannah to the end of her rope. She held the pieces of her broken heart up to the Lord in surrender.

"O LORD of Heaven's Armies, if you will look upon my sorrow and answer my prayer and give me a son, then I will give him back to you. He will be yours for his entire lifetime" (1 Samuel 1:11).

Reflect on what happened in *God's* timing.

Hannah drew close to the Lord. She prayed fervently. She came to a point where she would give back to God the son she so desperately longed to hold. God's timing brought Hannah to a point at which she could open her arms and give God the exact, perfect servant He required. And, she encountered Eli, a man who would recognize the incredible gift God had given her son Samuel.

Looking back, we see God's hand skillfully orchestrating every aspect of Hannah's and Samuel's lives—in *His* time.

Hannah shares God's waiting room with some pretty noble company. Scripture abounds with accounts of people who experienced the difficulty of operating on God's timetable.

Abram waited nearly a *century* for God to give him the promised descendant (Genesis 12–21).

Joseph sat in prison, biding his time until the dreams God had given him came to pass (Genesis 37–41).

David was a teenage boy when Samuel anointed him as Israel's king . . . but he didn't take the throne until he was probably in his thirties (1 Samuel 16–2 Samuel 2).

For decades, Zechariah thought his wife, Elizabeth, was barren. Then Gabriel told him she'd bear a son to be named John in her old age (Luke 1).

Simeon watched day after day, nearly his entire life, for the Christ, as promised to him by the Holy Spirit (Luke 2:25–32).

God needed each of these people to wait for his plans and timing to be just right.

Years ago, I had a lengthy layover on an international flight. Normally this meant I'd have to find an overpriced granola bar at a newsstand, then search for a less-grimy corner of the airport floor where I could camp out for a few hours. If I could be near a bathroom and a power outlet, it would seem miraculous. But on this trip I was with a coworker who traveled frequently and had access to the VIP lounge. Wow! Talk about a *great* way to spend a few hours! Plush armchairs and footrests, luxurious bathrooms (with showers!), free food and drinks, a library of newspapers and magazines. The hours breezed by in comfort.

As our friends struggle through the wait, what if we viewed our prayers as a spiritual "VIP waiting room" for them? Could we possibly pray this kind of comfort and peace around them?

A great waiting area has soft, cozy chairs.

Lord, bring comfort and peace to my friend's heart. Let her rest in the warmth of your love.

It's easy to wait when there are snacks and food.

Jesus, feed my friend with your Word. Let your words nourish her and give her the spiritual nutrition and energy she needs.

Hmm, you've got to have a bathroom nearby.

Heavenly Father, as my friend waits for your timing, give her all she needs physically.

Books, magazines, TV—those all make the wait easier to bear.

God, show me how I can bring joy to my friend as she endures this season. Give us opportunities to laugh together. Help my words to be life-giving.

Some of our loved ones are in for a long, long wait. God's timing isn't ours. God's timing may even stretch beyond our lifetime.

In 1882, a Catalan architect named Antoni Gaudi inherited a recently started project. A simple temple in Barcelona, dedicated to the Holy Family. As an architect, Gaudi found his inspiration in nature, praising and preferring God's designs seen through creation. He envisioned the temple as something grander than the original plan. This glorious tribute to the life of Christ had to be jaw-dropping. And he understood that something this majestic would never be accomplished in his lifetime. He would never see the completion of the vision. That didn't seem to worry Gaudi, whose goal was simply to create something that honored the Creator. "My client is not in a hurry," he quipped. And La Sagrada Familia was *still* under construction as of 2018.[1]

God's timing isn't ours. It transcends the boundaries of hours, days, birth and death. Jesus's closest friends couldn't comprehend God's eternal timeline, either. When Jesus rose from the dead, they likely assumed that things would change for God's people. After all, the promised Messiah and conquering king was here, right?

"So when the apostles were with Jesus, they kept asking him, 'Lord, has the time come for you to free Israel and restore our kingdom?' He replied, 'The Father alone has the authority to set those dates and times, and they are not for you to know'" (Acts 1:6–7).

As frustrating as it is to wait for God's timing, we have the reassurance that the one who holds our future does so with loving hands. Just as Antoni Gaudi envisioned something grand and inspiring, God's plans are beyond our wildest dreams. They may even extend beyond our lives on this earth. Let the pause bring us peace, as we entrust the blueprints to the skillful hands of a creative and caring heavenly Father.

PRAY TODAY

Find a piece of string and think of someone who's at the end of his or her rope—like Hannah. Tie a knot and ask God to give you the words to help that person hang on until His time is right.

CHAPTER 4

BEING THE VOICE

Samuel snored softly and turned over on his mat. Another busy day of serving Eli had left the preteen exhausted.

"Samuel!"

The voice that broke through his dreams sounded a little familiar. In his foggy, sleep-clouded brain, the boy assumed old Eli needed something. He rubbed his eyes, then scrambled to his feet and padded into the priest's bedroom.

"Yes?" Samuel replied. "What is it? Did you call me?"

Eli startled awake, with a groan and a grumble. "I didn't call you," Eli replied. "Go back to bed."

Samuel shrugged, then shuffled back down the hall. *Maybe Eli's just talking in his sleep*, he thought, flopping down and trying to find a comfortable spot.

"Samuel!"

This time, he *knew* he'd heard something! Samuel dutifully got back up and tiptoed to Eli's room, gently rousing the old man.

"Here I am. Did you call me?"

Eli ran a hand over his weary face. Getting a good night's sleep at his age was hard enough without this overeager servant interrupting!

"I didn't call you, my son. Go back to bed."

Samuel scratched his head and frowned. This was getting weird! He shook his head and slipped back to his mat and stretched out. This time, he listened.

"Samuel!"

The boy paused, feeling a little silly. But who else would be calling him at this hour of the night? Was someone playing a joke? Whatever it was, maybe Eli would know. So Samuel set off once more for the priest's bedroom. He hesitated, and gulped.

"Here I am. Did you call me?"

When Eli opened his eyes, Samuel caught a glimmer there. The old man put his hand on Samuel's tousled head.

"Go and lie down again," he said "and if someone calls again, say, 'Speak, LORD, your servant is
listening.'"

Dazed and confused, Samuel obeyed, opening
his ears to God's voice. When God spoke again,
the message he shared probably wasn't what the
boy expected—or hoped to hear. God spoke of a
harsh punishment against Eli and his wicked sons,
who'd blasphemed God. God detailed severe consequences that made Samuel shudder. We can only
imagine the boy's sleepless night, wrestling with
how to share the news with Eli. Samuel had spent
his entire childhood serving the elderly priest, and
now he had to share a message of misery with him?

In the morning, Eli saw the hesitation on the
boy's face, and demanded to know what God had
said. So Samuel spilled the beans, telling *everything*. We don't know what the worrisome news
stirred in Eli's heart, but he accepted God's message stoically.

"'It is the LORD's will,' Eli replied. 'Let him do
what he thinks best'" (1 Samuel 3:18).

As difficult as it might have been to share God's
message, Samuel faithfully obeyed. In adulthood
he became one of Israel's most powerful leaders,
sharing messages from God, guiding the Israelites,
praying for them, even selecting their first kings.

Prayer turns our hearts toward God. And sometimes God uses *our* attentive hearts to share a message for a loved one. Remember hitting the scan button on your car radio, listening intently so you knew when to stop and tune in to something you'd like? Well, when we shift our attention, thoughts, passions, and time toward the Lord, we find ourselves tuned in to hear from God as well. And like Samuel, you may not even expect it!

My friend Steve didn't expect the message he heard from God one Sunday in church. Oh, of course he'd hoped to hear from God at church . . . but this message was a bit puzzling. As Steve enjoyed praise and worship that morning in his usual pew, he glanced at the man standing in front of him. When Steve looked at him, he felt a sharp pain in his lower back. But when Steve looked away, the pain left. This happened a few times.

"OK, God," Steve prayed, "I get the message."

He took a hard look at the guy, and this time there was no pain for Steve, but the man in front of him shuffled back and forth on his feet like his back was killing him.

Steve says, "I felt like the Holy Spirit said to me, 'I want you to pray for him, but I'm not going to heal him today.' I was hoping that maybe I wasn't hearing God correctly, but the thought didn't change."

During the "meet and greet time" after worship, Steve set aside his embarrassment, mustered his courage, and approached the stranger. He introduced himself, and the man said his name was Josh.

"So Josh," Steve asked, "what's wrong with your back?"

Josh was a little surprised, but explained that he had an injury to his lower back, and that he'd been living with constant pain for a long time. Steve told him, "I feel like God wants me to pray for you, but I also feel like God isn't going to heal you today." He asked if it was OK to pray anyway. Josh said yes, so Steve prayed what felt like an amateurish appeal for Josh's back. Then they both went back to the rest of the church service.

After church, Josh stopped Steve, saying, "I just want you to know that God did what He intended, what I needed, when you prayed for me. Whether I'm healed or not, God did what I needed. Thank you for being willing to step out in faith and pray for me."

Steve muses, "I have no idea what 'God did.' Maybe Josh just needed to know God was still listening? That God cared about his pain? I don't know. There was no healing, but something happened in Josh's heart anyway, and whatever it was seemed to be enough for him."[1]

Like Samuel, Steve wished he had an uplifting, positive, hopeful word from God. Instead, he had to be the bearer of a difficult truth. Yet because God knew the circumstances, the message was perfect and served its purpose.

Occasionally God allows us to be His messenger—the voice that a friend will hear. As we intercede on behalf of our loved ones, God may send us a specific word, most often a Scripture or Bible promise, to share with them. God's messages can be encouraging. Or they might be difficult. They may even be downright puzzling. But you can bet that they'll nearly *always* push us out of our comfort zone.

Take a minute and try something. Fold your hands, as if you're getting ready to pray, then look at your thumbs, which are probably crossed over each other. Note which thumb is on top. Now, switch thumb positions, so the *opposite* thumb is on top. How does that feel? Why?

When we pray for friends, sometimes God asks us to do something that feels awkward, unnatural, or uncomfortable. It's not the way we usually do things.

Perhaps God has nudged you to pray for someone, right in the moment.

Really, God? What if people are watching? What if the person says no?

You may have felt God prompt you to share a Scripture, blessing, or prayer with someone you don't know.

Oh, I can't do that! I'd be so embarrassed! What would I even say?

And how would you respond if God gave you a mysterious—or hard-to-bear—message for a friend?

Are you sure you need me to do this, Lord? What will they think?

Being a messenger for the Lord may sound grand, but it can feel goofy. Just ask my friend, Karl.

Karl and I worked together, but lost touch for several years when he moved his family across the state. So I was surprised when he called one morning, with a bit of an embarrassed stammer and pause in his voice.

"I woke up this morning with a clear sense that I'm supposed to share this message from God with you. This is super weird and I have no idea what it means. But God does and maybe you will, too. So I'm just going to be obedient and go for it."

Well, my curiosity was piqued . . . and it honestly felt kind of cool that God had a message for me! What if it's something life-changing? What if it sends me across the globe on a new adventure? With my mind racing into exciting corners of the world, I urged Karl to share it with me.

"God is telling you to do the right thing," he said. Huh.

I'll be honest, the words didn't have earth-shattering, pieces-falling-into-place meaning for me at the time. I pondered why God would have that message for me—in my work, friendships, marriage, and parenting. And I kind of felt embarrassed. Would my friend take this to mean that I *wasn't* doing the right thing in some area of my life? I mean, "do the right thing" is definitely a godly, biblical truth. But I wasn't at a point where I'd been tempted to do anything unethical or immoral. Yet, for *years* those words—that message for me from my heavenly Father—have stuck with me. To this day, I think of them frequently. That phrase rings in my ears as I make choices at work and at home. I have no idea what decisions they've influenced, and what relationships they've altered. I'm thankful for the faithful courage of my friend, to set aside his self-consciousness and the awkwardness of the moment, and share a message from God—for me.

When we commit to interceding in prayer with a friend, we usually envision the warm fuzzies—lifting up the burden of a loved one, kneeling with a heartbroken neighbor, or coming alongside a faltering family member. We may not bargain for awkwardness, risk, or sharing something they don't want to hear. This is where our deep friendship with God, our obedience to *His* wisdom and sovereignty, take over. When God speaks, we take a deep breath, set aside our pride and will, and exchange them for the honor of playing a part in his mystery.

Even Jesus wrestled with doing things God's way. In the Garden of Gethsemane, He cried out, "My Father! If it is possible, let this cup of suffering be taken away from me. Yet I want your will to be done, not mine" (Matthew 26:39). *The Message* translation puts it closer to the way you and I might express our discomfort:

> My Father, if there is any way, get me out of this. But please, not what I want. You, what do *you* want?

Moses resisted God's call for him to share an unpopular message with a powerful Pharaoh. When God appeared in a burning bush, and gave Moses the task of being his mouthpiece to Pharaoh and the Israelites, Moses balked:

> But Moses protested again, "What if they won't believe me or listen to me? What if they say, 'The LORD never appeared to you'?" (Exodus 4:1)

Jesus faced torture and death. Moses risked the wrath of Pharaoh.

What's at risk for us if we step out and share an awkward or unpopular message?

What if my friend thinks I'm being weird or judgmental?

What if my family member gets mad?

What if I look ridiculous?

What if people stare?

What if I'm wrong?

First, if you feel you have a message from God, it's essential to *always* compare it to Scripture. God never tells us to do anything outside of who He is, and we understand His nature through His Word. Don't skip this step!

Next, pray for God's wisdom in *how* you share the message. Approach your loved one with grace, gentleness, and humility. Be honest! It's OK to admit that this feels uncomfortable or you're not sure what this message even means. Your vulnerability and candor will help level the playing field and create common ground between you and the recipient.

Lastly, set aside your worry about what everyone else will think. This is between you and God—not you and everyone sitting in the coffee shop who might be watching. God has chosen *you*—for a reason only He knows—to bear a heavenly message. You have what it takes!

Welcome the honor.

Embrace your role.

Thank God for allowing you to be a part of His plans.

You have the voice.

Do you have the heart?

PRAY TODAY

Remember when you switched your "praying thumbs" earlier in this chapter? Let's try that again. Fold your hands in prayer and take a look at your thumbs. Switch their position so they feel unnatural and uncomfortable. Now pray, asking God to give you the courage to step out of your comfort zone. Listen quietly, opening your heart to receive any words God needs to share with you. It might be a sense, a word, or a picture. If the message is related to a friend or family member, set aside your awkwardness and fear. Exchange those emotions and worries for the honor of being used to share a heavenly message with a hurting heart.

CHAPTER 5

LANGUAGE
OF THE HEART

Mary Poppins had an answer for everything. When she needed a hat stand, she simply pulled one from her bottomless carpetbag. When Uncle Albert got stuck on the ceiling, she knew that telling him something sad would get him down. When Jane and Michael wouldn't take their medicine, she had the exact song to make them comply.

She even knew what to say when you didn't know what to say:

Supercalifragilisticexpialidocious.

If only it was always that simple.[1]

There are times in life when we honestly don't know the right thing to say. How do you respond when a loved one tells you they're getting a divorce? What words can you use when a friend tells you he lost his job? Is there any possible thing to say when someone tells you the chemo didn't work? Grief, uncertainty, loss, and heartache leave us at a loss for words.

Sometimes we aren't even sure how to verbalize our anguish as we pray—and we aren't the first to feel that way:

> I am exhausted and completely crushed. My groans come from an anguished heart. You know what I long for, Lord; you hear my every sigh. (Psalm 38:8–9)

> I call to God; God will help me. At dusk, dawn, and noon I sigh deep sighs—he hears, he rescues. (Psalm 55:16 MSG)

It's a good thing we serve a God who's fluent in groans and sighs, isn't it? There are times when words can't express the depth of our ache. We aren't sure what to ask for because we're overwhelmed by a crushing tidal wave of pain or confusion or disbelief.

I've been there.

"Jody, it's cancer."

The choked sob at the other end of the phone belonged to my sister and best friend, Amy. This had to be a mistake. Amy—healthy, vibrant, young, full of joy and life? I quickly discovered that cancer isn't selective or practical or kind or gracious. It invades relentlessly.

I can think of a thousand words to describe my beautiful sister. I can think of a thousand words to describe cancer. But I can't begin to verbalize the kind of grief I experienced as my sister began her slow journey into the arms of Jesus. The English language is pitifully inadequate at describing the depth of loss, the pain, the helplessness of watching a loved one die.

Amy's otherwise-healthy body was reluctant to give up its fight. For months, family members took turns staying with her in the hospital or at home. I usually took the morning shift when Amy was in the hospital, relieving my dad who'd slept on a cot in Amy's room.

I can't count the mornings I sat in that hospital chair, watching my beloved sister take her final breaths. More times than not, my prayers were wordless. I don't mean that I prayed silently, pouring out coherent requests to God. I simply couldn't wrap my head around what was happening, let alone my words. Prayer became inner groans, sighs, or concentrated emotion. I steeped my heart in God— just soaking in His presence and releasing pain, need, confusion, and frustration. Sometimes I'd manage one word, prayed again and again for hours.

Comfort.

Peace.

Heal.

Wholeness.

Mercy.

Jesus.

I relied on Paul's wisdom to the Christians in Rome:

> But the Holy Spirit prays for us with groanings that cannot be expressed in words. And the Father who knows all hearts knows what the Spirit is saying, for the Spirit pleads for us believers in harmony with God's own will. (Romans 8:26–27)

I found comfort in the truth that I had a Father who "knows all hearts."

Praying for loved ones *isn't* about having all the right words to say. It's about admitting that our heart has a language only God knows . . . and that's OK. Communication and intercession can be a communion of spirits—ours with the Holy Spirit. Sometimes we simply need to abide in Jesus and let Him carry our heart's message to the Father. *He* knows the words our hearts struggle to find.

Wordless prayer isn't just for times of heartbreak or sadness. Joy is sometimes inexpressible! Have you ever witnessed a "God moment," a peek into heaven that left you wide-eyed in wonder? Perhaps the first time you saw the Grand Canyon your jaw dropped and you felt an overwhelming sense of love for our creative Lord. Or when you held your child or grand-child your heart bent with a breathtaking perspective of God's love. It may have been a moment during worship when the spirit of community with other Christians took your breath—and words—away. Those are times when our soul reaches out to God in wordless awe, and we simply *are*. When Hannah held little Samuel, she prayed, "My heart rejoices in the LORD!" (1 Samuel 2:1). We can imagine Hannah's broken heart melting back together with a flood of love, gratitude, wonder, and joy.

Wordless communion with God, whether in anguish or awe, is beautiful.

How precious to realize that we don't even need words to share our hearts with Jesus! There's an intimacy with such expression, knitting our spirit with that of our Creator.

People communicate with dots and dashes, flags, smoke signals, whistles, sign language, and body language. Why should our conversations with Christ be limited to an English language that contains only around 250,000 words?[2] God, the creator of heaven and earth, time and space—the God who was and is and is to come—isn't constrained by such a relatively small number of ways to express emotion! Author and theologian C. S. Lewis saw tremendous value in a "wordless" prayer that connects us with the heart of God:

> I tried to pray without words at all—not to verbalize the mental acts. Even in praying for others I believe I tended to avoid their names and substituted mental images of them. I still think that the prayer without words is the best—if one can really achieve it.[3]

However, there may be times when you *want* to put words to what you're feeling as you commune with God. Maybe you need to get some language around your thoughts, or sort through what you're feeling. Let me suggest the idea of praying Scripture. The powerful practice of praying Scripture during those moments can allow God's Word to become *your* words. Praying Scripture goes beyond simply reciting Bible passages we've memorized. It's speaking the words *and* the truths they hold in the context of our situation. Praying Scripture states the bedrock of God's Word, and can give us a solid perspective when emotion knocks us off our feet.

As a young girl, Psalm 121 became a favorite piece of Scripture for me. It's one that comes to mind easily. Frequently as I sat beside Amy, holding her hand, I'd look out her hospital window at a stunning view of the Rocky Mountains, which always reminded me of the first phrase of that Psalm, "I lift my eyes to the mountains." And my prayers sounded a bit like this:

> *Jesus, as I look at these incredible mountains, I know that my help comes from you—the one who crafted those mighty mountains. The hands that were powerful enough to shape rock are gentle enough to hold my sister as she suffers. You, who love me and love Amy, are our help. You're present in this awful moment. You're watching over Amy. You're not sleeping or letting us stumble through this. You're her protection from the relentless pain—both inside and out. Please shield her from any more pain. Day and night, you're watching over Amy. She's never alone. You've promised to be with us now and forevermore,*

*and I'm so thankful for the promise you've given
Amy of a forevermore with you in heaven.*

Praying Scripture reminds us that Christ is close
to us when despair makes Him seem distant. God's
Word reflects His promises when pain eclipses His
presence. Speaking truths about God and His char-
acter point to who He is when life overwhelms us.

Sometimes words fail us. They're small and frail
and limiting. What a joy to know that God speaks
fluent groans, sighs, silence, and murmurings. We
can draw close to a mighty God who doesn't need
structured phrases, nouns, verbs, and adjectives.

He always hears an open heart.

PRAY TODAY

Not sure what to pray? Sit and steep your
heart in God. Absorb His power and love,
releasing back your emotion to Him. It's OK
if you don't have words! Remember, your Lord
speaks the language of the heart. If you want
to give words to your emotions, find a quiet
place to pray Scripture back to God. To make
it easy, choose a Psalm—most of these are out-
pourings of emotion from David's heart. Let

God's Word guide your heart, aligning it with His. When a passage says "I," insert your own name, or the name of the person you're praying for. Thank God for the truths about Him that you find in that passage.

CHAPTER 6

CARRYING HOPE

It seemed like an appealing idea to any curious kid. After practice, twelve boys from a Thai soccer team thought it might be fun to explore the nearby caves of Tham Luang. The team frequently spent time together outside of the game, and this would be another exciting adventure with a group of friends. With their coach, the kids (ranging in age from eleven to fourteen) hiked and climbed and splashed through the underground tunnels for about an hour. When they turned around to head home, their sense of adventure was soon replaced with a sense of dread. Everything had changed.

Water had poured into the tunnel, blocking off their exit. And the water was steadily rising.

Coach Ake led the team to higher ground, farther back in the cave. He hoped the waters might recede overnight . . . but when the kids awoke to the sound of flowing water, the gravity of the situation became all too real. For nine long days, the boys lived in darkness. Although they tried to keep each other's spirits up, hopelessness rose along with the creeping waterline. Empty stomachs rumbled and fearful thoughts tumbled through their minds. How would they ever get out? Without food, could they even stay alive until the floodwaters receded? Things looked black and bleak.

On the tenth day, they thought they heard voices—but how? Coach Ake told the boys to be quiet and they all listened in the dark. Just above the sound of flowing water . . . voices! But these voices didn't speak Thai. Two British cave divers emerged from the water, catching the team by surprise. The boys learned that the world had been watching and waiting, furiously trying to figure out a way to free them. Wild attempts had been made at pumping water from the caves, and divers had explored the best possible ways to reach them. While a group of desperate boys huddled in the dismal blackness of a cave, thousands of volunteers scrambled to save them. Those two voices brought a message of rescue, hope, and love.[1]

Do you know someone who's in a cave of despair right now? Is there a loved one who's sitting in the shadows, wondering if there's any way out? Maybe you can picture that family member so deep in distress that any light seems desperately out of reach.

Perhaps God is calling *you* to be the voice they hear in the dark. Through prayer, we get to bring joy and hope, the truth of God's love, to our fear-focused friends and family members. As we pray for others, we can ask God for *His* words of love to share with them. Your voice can bear God's precious, life-giving, sustaining words to someone who only hears what they fear.

Solomon grasped the power of encouraging words:

Gentle words are a tree of life. (Proverbs 15:4)

The words of the godly are a life-giving fountain. (Proverbs 10:11)

The lips of the godly speak helpful words. (Proverbs 10:32)

This goes beyond merely throwing out a few helpful or kind words to friends. While God *does* call us to encourage one another, interceding for others gives God a chance to speak *to* us, then *through* us to those who need *His* encouragement.

Try something with me. Read through this experience, then set your book down and take a couple minutes to try it on your own.

Envision Jesus sitting with you. What does He look like? (Maybe Jesus isn't dressed in robes today. After all, He only wore those because that's what everyone else was wearing back in the day. What might He wear if he came to your house today?) Now, think of a friend who could use a word from Jesus. Imagine that friend beside you, too. Set your phone timer for one minute. Ask Jesus "Do you have a word for my friend, (name)? What hopeful word can I share with her (or him)? I only want to hear from you, Lord." Sit silently and listen for one full minute. (Although you don't have to close your eyes, it might help to block out distraction if you do.)

Got it? Now, pause and try the experience.

What happened? What did that feel like?

God may give you one word, an image, a sense, or even Scripture. God may give you peace or silence. God may not have any specific message for that friend today—and that's OK, too!

A leader shared this activity recently in a group setting while I was there. We paired up with a friend, and the leader asked individuals to envision Jesus sitting with them. After a pause, we asked Jesus for a word about our partner. What did He want to tell them? What picture did He have for them? We waited the full, long, silent minute. As I did this with my friend Kelsey in mind, I had a clear picture of Jesus beside me. When I asked Him what He wanted to tell me about Kelsey, the image was as clear as day: Jesus's face lit up—like someone seeing a loved one or a gift set before them.

"Kelsey? I *love* her! I'm so pleased with her."

What a joy to share this with my friend! We both had tears in our eyes as we soaked in Jesus's love. The encouragement didn't come *from* me, but *through* me, to the heart of this child of God. Our heavenly Father knows when we need a word of hope, doesn't He?

After the crucifixion of their master, Jesus's friends were at their lowest point. For years they'd abandoned careers, families, and homes to follow Jesus. They'd believed His message, witnessed His miracles, and taken His mission to be their own calling. And now, in the blink of an eye, it was over. At the foot of the cross they'd even heard Jesus himself utter the words "It is finished." *That* didn't sound very hopeful or victorious. Not only had they lost a beloved leader, they'd become outlaws on the run from a triumphant troop of Pharisees. The future looked grim. Their cave of despair must have seemed large enough to swallow them whole. And then . . . a message *to* the men, *through* the women:

> The women ran quickly from the tomb. They were very frightened but also filled with great joy, and they rushed to give the disciples the angel's message. And as they went, Jesus met them and greeted them. And they ran to him, grasped his feet, and worshiped him. Then Jesus said to them, "Don't be afraid! Go tell my brothers to leave for Galilee, and they will see me there." (Matthew 28:8–10)

Can you imagine the fun of being those women, getting to be the voice of joy and truth that would break through the men's misery? What a delight to carry Jesus's message *to* them, *for* them, *about* them! As you seek the Lord on behalf of a friend, allow Him to use *you* to carry His message of hope. Look for opportunities to shine God's love into someone's life. It might mean delivering a divine message, but most likely it'll be simply reminding a friend of the solid truths we trust in Scripture.

In the bleakness of depression or discouragement, it's easy to only hear the negative. Sometimes misery plugs our ears and blinds our heart to the life-giving reality of God's love and power. In the gloom, God's voice can seem silent. You've experienced a bit of this if you've ever asked for feedback about a project you worked on. Twenty people raved about it, but that *one* bit of negative criticism is what stuck in your head . . . right? We block out the good and only hear the bad.

Stressors (including negative comments) actually affect our brains! Research shows that even a few days of stress impacts how well the neurons in the hippocampus work. The hippocampus, that part of the brain responsible for reasoning and memory, starts to act a little less effectively. After a long time, the impact on the neurons is actually irreparable![2] So your role in bringing God's joy and *truth* to a friend is critically important. Consider yourself a brain surgeon, restoring life to that confused hippocampus!

As you tune your ears and heart toward God in an effort to listen for a message, it's a good idea to find time alone where it's quiet. Even Jesus—God incarnate—needed to get away from it all to listen to the heavenly Father.

Before daybreak the next morning, Jesus got up and went out to an isolated place to pray. (Mark 1:35)

Early the next morning Jesus went out to an isolated place. The crowds searched everywhere for him, and when they finally found him, they begged him not to leave them. (Luke 4:42)

But Jesus often withdrew to the wilderness for prayer. (Luke 5:16)

Time alone must have been a rare, treasured gift for Jesus. Once news of His miracles and radical teaching got out, everyone clamored for His time and attention. Scripture repeatedly records Jesus trying to get away, but being followed and found by desperate crowds.

I imagine you have days that feel like that, too. We're busier now than ever, and carving out a few minutes to simply be still before the Lord, to listen and wait, to abide in Him . . . that's hard! We often feel guilty for setting aside time for ourselves when others seem to need us or we've made commitments. But, friend, consider this: those moments with God just may be what He needs in order to whisper into your ear a much-needed word of encouragement for someone else. The time that *seems* to be for you *just might* be for a friend in need. If it was a priority for Jesus, you can bet it should be a priority for us, too. And even if God doesn't have a word for a friend, your soul may need the comfort of simply abiding in Christ for a few minutes.

Too many of our friends are like that Thai soccer team, waiting in the dark. They feel lost and alone, distant from God's loving care. They're watching the floods of fear rising, and their faith grows faint. Your voice, bearing God's message of hope and love, might be the life-giving truth they desperately need to hear.

PRAY TODAY

Commit to the "one-minute listening experience" every day this week. Keeping a specific friend in mind, ask God to let you hear only from Him, and to give you a Scripture, picture, or message about that friend. Then wait patiently with Jesus.

CHAPTER 7

SMALL SHIPS

Nine days.
That's approximately 216 hours. Or 12,960 minutes, if you're counting.

Private Tommy Brabban probably counted every single one of them as he huddled under an ambulance, enduring days of smoke, noise, fear, death, confusion, and hunger. In late May 1940, Tommy and his unit joined the frenzied throng of more than four hundred thousand British, French, and Belgian troops on the beaches of Dunkirk, France. Hitler's forces had cut off their escape to the south, causing a mass evacuation along the northern coast of France. As the Luftwaffe strafed the beaches, soldiers scrambled to board any military ships they could reach in hopes of escaping across the channel to Dover.

William Reeves describes the horrific scene on the beach: "Dunkirk was noise and chaos. There was black smoke blowing over the place, there were aeroplanes coming over and dropping bombs. Huge crowds of people were moving towards the docks, thousands of soldiers were on the beach."[1]

Freedom wouldn't come easily.

"We were wading out to this boat and some German planes came over and they bombed the boat. They bombed everything that was around. One of these bombs went down the funnel of this boat—we at least thought it looked very much like that. It just went bang. And that was it. Our transport home had gone."[2]

Tommy's unit—and hundreds just like it—survived on the beach for more than a week. Luftwaffe bombings kept everyone on edge and in danger. The staggering number of men needing to flee left the Royal Navy shorthanded. How could they ever evacuate nearly half a *million* men before the German attack intensified? As if things weren't grim enough, air attacks damaged the dock that took men into the harbor where the large ships could meet them. Now the ships that *were* large enough to accommodate so many men simply couldn't reach the shallow beaches. Men tried to swim out to the ships . . . and drowned.

The enemy drew near. Food grew scarce. Rescue seemed impossible.

Trapped on the beach with no escape, soldiers like Tommy prayed for a miracle.

It came in the form of something small. Well, a *lot* of small somethings.

Little fishing boats, trawlers, pleasure craft— they came by the hundreds. Piloted by fishermen and civilian sailors, grandfathers and teenage boys, these became lifelines for hundreds of thousands of men. The unlikely crews dodged bullets and bombs, risking their lives to carry stranded soldiers to the safety of larger ships or to ferry them all the way to the Dover shore. Cecilia Sandys, grand-daughter of Winston Churchill, says the "small ships" possibly changed the course of the war. And likely history.

"My grandfather was only expecting 30,000 to be brought back . . . and they brought back over 360,000 men. And if that hadn't happened, we'd probably be flying the German flag today." Working together, that unassuming armada became a mighty force.[3]

Listen to me now: *Prayer works the same way.*

You may feel like a "small ship" as you pray with a friend who's facing a tidal wave of heartache. The problem looks overwhelming, and your cries to God seem insufficient. But there's power when we mobilize forces around a common cause! It's not necessarily that our prayers become more powerful, or that God requires more prayers before He acts. God hears and responds to *every* prayer—from a tiny whisper to a passionate petition. But something happens within *us*—and within those we're praying for—when we join together in prayer. Unity creates an unstoppable sense of community that has far-reaching impact.

The early church gives us a beautiful picture of what happens when Christians unite in prayer. Let's drop in on them at this crucial, memorable moment. Jesus had just ascended to heaven, leaving His followers the task—and joy—of spreading the message of God's love and Jesus's salvation. Think of these men and women as pioneers setting foot in a new land. They relied on each other to navigate unexplored territory, find their footing, embrace change, and stay strong during intense persecution. So it's no wonder that we read this in Acts 1, regarding that first small group of apostles: "They all met together and were constantly united in prayer . . ." (Acts 1:14).

Can you imagine what corporate prayer meant to that little band of believers? Try to fathom what it did to their spirits, hearing friendly voices lifting up the name of Jesus. Prayer meant that they weren't alone on this new venture. Not only did prayer remind them of Jesus's power, it emboldened their hearts as one! Each believer knew that he or she was part of a body—a team. As they prayed and petitioned aloud, the unspoken undercurrent whispered, "We're in this together. You're not alone. I've got your back!" After the Holy Spirit came at Pentecost, the number of followers swelled . . . and communal prayer *continued* to be a cornerstone of their faith family.

> All the believers devoted themselves to the apostles' teaching, and to fellowship, and to sharing in meals (including the Lord's Supper), and to prayer. (Acts 2:42)

Prayer unified the first followers, and it can unify us today as we join voices. The first Christians had their lives at stake, which drove them to their knees together. There was urgency and hunger for God's direction, divine protection, and human connection. These are the moments in which corporate prayer is at its most potent, because it transforms the ones *praying* and the one being prayed *for*.

The book of Esther is unique in that it doesn't ever mention the name of God. However, we can see God's hand, and a passion *for* God, through the story of this Jewish girl who became queen. It probably seemed like smooth sailing for Esther after the whirlwind selection process she'd been through. She'd finally been crowned Queen of Persia. Wow . . . and whew!

Then a knock at her royal chamber door.

Cousin Mordecai sent an urgent message filled with ominous news about the destruction of Esther's people. Men, women, and children would be massacred out of spite and revenge . . . and all for a bit of silver. Mordecai implored Esther to approach the king and beg for mercy, for her *and* for her people.

> Don't think for a moment that because you're in the palace you will escape when all other Jews are killed. If you keep quiet at a time like this, deliverance and relief for the Jews will arise from some other place, but you and your relatives will die. Who knows if perhaps you were made queen for just such a time as this? (Esther 4:13–14)

Esther hesitated. Approaching the king without being summoned could cost her life! Yet, if she didn't speak up, she *and* thousands of people would die.

> Go and gather together all the Jews of Susa and fast for me. Do not eat or drink for three days, night or day. My maids and I will do the same. And then, though it is against the law, I will go in to see the king. (Esther 4:16)

Esther rallies her people—like the small ships at Dunkirk—to carry her burden and lay it before God. While the passage doesn't specify prayer, Matthew Henry's commentary gives this insight about Esther's decision: "She believed that God's favour was to be obtained by prayer, that His people are a praying people, and He a prayer-hearing God. She knew it was the practice of good people, in extraordinary cases, to join fasting with prayer, and many of them to join together in both."[4]

With so much at stake, Esther joined with her people. We can imagine a nation on its knees, pouring out petitions for mercy, favor, and miracles. Esther knew she wasn't alone. The people trusted they had a champion willing to give her life for them. For three days, prayers and fasting unified a queen and her people.

Corporate prayer creates a community for today's faith family, too. Unified prayer knits our hearts as we experience struggles and successes as one.

Jessica learned this firsthand this when she and her husband, Dale, moved to a new town. This young couple, expecting their first baby, had just settled into a local church yet felt far from family and dear friends. Jessica admits they didn't know many people in the church. But when the doctor suspected something wasn't right with the baby, she knew enough to ask for prayer—even from strangers. At thirty weeks pregnant, Jessica found herself flat on her back in a hospital bed, with orders to stay there for five weeks! Feelings of fear, isolation, and uncertainty crept in during those long, lonely weeks. The pastor of their new church visited, as well as immediate family from out of state. They asked their church family to pray, but since they didn't really know many people, the young couple didn't give the request much thought. After inducing labor, doctors delivered baby Derek, safe and healthy. Jessica and Dale thanked God for answering prayers with such a precious blessing. But God's blessings continued.

"After Derek was born, and we were finally able to take our preemie out to meet the world, I met so many people at church who were so excited to meet the baby they had prayed for," Jessica reflects. "It was beautiful. Years later, I was reminded that a sweet nurse at our church had visited me, prayed and checked on our progress during those five weeks . . . when she was, by random chance, assigned as Derek's VBS crew leader! She was overjoyed to get to know the baby (now kid) she had prayed for and see the amazing things God had done through Derek."[5]

Communal prayer touched the heart of a new mom, brought a healthy baby into the world, and *years later* showed the intricate way that God works at bringing people together. Jessica and Dale discovered the warmth of a thriving, caring faith family who became a part of their lives for years to come. And today Jessica views this experience as evidence of God's hand on her son's life. All because many small ships came together to carry the burdens of a single frightened young woman.

During his ministry, the apostle Paul faced starvation, storms, shipwreck, prison, and beatings. Like those battered soldiers at Dunkirk, he called on his prayer armada for rescue.

Dear brothers and sisters, I urge you in the name of our Lord Jesus Christ to join in my struggle by praying to God for me. Do this because of your love for me, given to you by the Holy Spirit. (Romans 15:30)

And you are helping us by praying for us. Then many people will give thanks because God has graciously answered so many prayers for our safety. (2 Corinthians 1:11)

Pray for us, too, that God will give us many opportunities to speak about his mysterious plan concerning Christ. That is why I am here in chains. Pray that I will proclaim this message as clearly as I should. (Colossians 4:3–4)

Finally, dear brothers and sisters, we ask you to pray for us. (2 Thessalonians 3:1)

These weren't offhand mentions of "keep me in your prayers." Paul relied on the life-saving, soul-reaching, unifying power of prayer. Not only did he treasure each voice lifting up his needs before Jesus, but that body of believers gave him the courage and heart to carry out a difficult mission. Fueled by Christ and supported by prayer, Paul's mission literally changed the course of human history worldwide.

Your boat may seem so small, and the ocean of ache so deep and wide.

But imagine the force of faith we could launch today.

Envision a unified team, lifting up and supporting each other in prayer.

It may take many small ships, but we can bring countless hearts to a safe harbor. So step in, sit down, and pick up the oars.

We've got a mission.

PRAY TODAY

Enlist a flotilla of faith! Today, reach out to a group of friends who will commit to joining with you around a particular area of prayer that's close to your heart. Connect weekly—in person, with texts, or via email—to pray together, share updates about what you're praying for, and perhaps even take some action toward the need that God has placed on your heart.

CHAPTER 8

RECEIVE
THE BLESSING

It took one tickle fight, two stuffed animals, three cups of water, and four songs, but three-year-old Anika was *finally* ready for bed. An exhausted Erik knelt beside his daughter's bed, folded his hands and bowed his head to pray with the preschooler.

Her sweet voice jumped in before he could begin.

"You can receive the blessing, Daddy."

"What?"

Anika took Erik's large hands in her pudgy ones, pressing them together and shaping his hands into a cup.

"Here. Now you're ready to receive the blessing. In Sunday school Miss Dee says we can pray like this."

Erik blinked back tears as his tiny daughter placed her open hands over his cupped hands and prayed for him. Anika's *words* weren't really any different that night, but Erik experienced prayer in a completely new way. He envisioned his heavenly Father placing blessings into his hands, and into his life. Ten years later, Erik still cups his hands during prayer in an expectant and thankful position before the Lord. "Receiving the blessing" gives Erik a fresh perspective on prayer, taking it from mere words to an act of communion and communication with God.

Prayer is more than words—it involves our heart and mind. Yet have you ever considered that prayer can involve your body, too? Of course you're familiar with a few prayer postures, such as bowing your head, folding your hands, and closing your eyes. Interestingly, Scripture never indicates that these are preferred or proper ways to present and prepare our bodies for prayer. A quick scan of the Bible shows us that people tended to be a bit more active in prayer!

Then Solomon stood before the altar of the LORD in front of the entire community of Israel. He lifted his hands toward heaven, and he prayed . . . (1 Kings 8:22)

But when Daniel learned that the law had been signed, he went home and knelt down as usual in his upstairs room, with its windows open toward Jerusalem. He prayed three times a day, just as he had always done, giving thanks to his God. (Daniel 6:10)

I fell to my knees and lifted my hands to the LORD my God. I prayed, "O my God, I am utterly ashamed." (Ezra 9:5–6)

He went on a little farther and bowed with his face to the ground, praying, "My Father! If it is possible, let this cup of suffering be taken away from me. Yet I want your will to be done, not mine." (Matthew 26:39)

The early church blessed its first leaders: "These seven were presented to the apostles, who prayed for them as they laid their hands on them." (Acts 6:6)

Connecting with God is an intimate, powerful moment, engaging mind, spirit, *and* body! Our postures, poses, actions, and gestures during prayer give depth to our conversations with Jesus. That's simply how God designed us.

Scientists tell us that bodies and brains are connected in countless ways. There's even a strong connection between our *emotions* and our bodies. In his book *Teaching with the Brain in Mind* Eric Jensen shares some of the brain research that sheds light on the link between our physical state and what's happening inside our bodies. Jensen states, "The part of the brain that processes movement is the same part of the brain that processes learning." He also affirms that "the relationship between movement and learning is so strong that it pervades all of life—and emotions are intertwined into the mix as well."[1]

So as we pour out our hearts to God, our bodies reflect or react to the emotions we're experiencing as well. Sometimes, these postures mirror our emotions almost subconsciously, such as when we fall to our knees in complete abandon before God. Other times, we may *choose* to take a posture that helps us better connect with an aspect of God. For example, praying with your eyes open, looking up at a stunning sunset allows you to enjoy your Creator. A prayerful posture can change *us* as we come before our heavenly Father. It may allow us to hear God in a fresh way, putting our heart in a right position before Him. Engaging physically can also put our *problems* in a right position—in God's hands!

That's what happened with King Hezekiah. Haven't heard of him? Let me introduce you!

Hezekiah trusted in the LORD, the God of Israel. There was no one like him among all the kings of Judah, either before or after his time. He remained faithful to the LORD in everything, and he carefully obeyed all the commands the LORD had given Moses. (2 Kings 18:5–6)

During his reign, Hezekiah revolted against the ungodly Assyrians, refusing to pay them tribute. Unfortunately, when they conquered Judah, the Assyrians weren't happy at this rebel king . . . so the Assyrian monarch, Sennacherib, set out to disgrace Hezekiah in front of his people.

Bible-times mudslinging was a lot like what you'd see today. Second Kings 18:19–37 gives us a good picture of all the tactics Sennacherib used:

Insults.

Threats.

Lies.

Slander.

Blasphemy against God.

When Sennacherib sent a scathing message, saying that God wouldn't protect Jerusalem, Hezekiah's response was to approach God in a unique way:

After Hezekiah received the letter from the messengers and read it, he went up to the

Lord's Temple and spread it out before the Lord. And Hezekiah prayed this prayer before the Lord . . . "Open your eyes, O Lord, and see! Listen to Sennacherib's words of defiance against the living God." (2 Kings 19:14–16)

What prayerful posture did Hezekiah take? He laid the offensive letters out before God, as if to say, "Do you see this, Lord? Look at these vile lies! Rescue us from such a godless nation." Of course God already knew the contents of the letter, but this wasn't about setting out the contents for God to read. Hezekiah actually laid his burden before God. He released it into God's hands as he cried out to his Father.

Are there things *you'd* like to physically lay before God? How would it change your prayer perspective to lay out the divorce papers as you cry out to Jesus? What would it be like to hold the doctor's report in your hands, showing it to the Lord? Would it feel any different if you printed out the gossip-filled email and held it out to your Father?

A physical demonstration or posture has the power to realign our hearts—*and our problems!* Those things can feel a bit smaller when we see them under the eye of the Creator. A sheet of paper might feel manageable in the hands of Christ. (By the way, to see how things turned out for Hezekiah, check out the rest of the story in 2 Kings 19.)

Engaging physically can enrich our experiences as we pray for our loved ones, too. My family once attended a church where, during baby dedication, the entire congregation extended a hand toward the new family as a form of blessing. Imagine the hearts of a young mom and dad as they see this entire congregation—their local family of God—physically reaching out to them in blessing and prayer. Perhaps you've put a hand of blessing on someone's head as you pray. What does that do to your heart? The heart of the recipient? Your physical touch may have allowed them to feel the loving hand of Jesus as you prayed.

Anthony Showalter, a music teacher in Alabama, came home from teaching one night to find two letters from former students. As his eyes pored over the words in the first letter, his heart ached for its writer, a young man from South Carolina who'd recently lost his wife. Anthony set aside the first letter and slowly opened the second. How could this be? A second young man *also* grieving the death of his wife! Anthony pondered, his heavy heart searching for any way to comfort and console these broken men in such a dark time. As usual, he turned to Scripture for solace. There, he came across Deuteronomy 33:27.

"The eternal God is your refuge, and his everlasting arms are under you."

The words stuck with him long after he'd responded to the students. He envisioned those everlasting arms as something mighty, something we could press into during difficult times. Taking up his pen and a fresh sheet of paper, Anthony began writing the chorus to what would become the beloved hymn, "Leaning on the Everlasting Arms."

Leaning, leaning,
Safe and secure from all alarms;
Leaning, leaning,
Leaning on the everlasting arms.[2]

"Leaning" is another posture of reliance—a picture and pose for prayer. Can you imagine leaning your head on a pillow, or your entire body against a wall, as you envision leaning on the arms of your Father? Engaging our bodies in prayer can bring hope and comfort when our spirits sag. And drawing our friends into this powerful practice, allowing them to experience God's presence, can change their hearts in mighty ways.

Open your hands, open your heart.
Lift your arms, lift your spirit.
Drop to your knees, and drop your pride.

Receive the blessing that God is eager to pour into your life.

PRAY TODAY

Think of something you've been praying about. What posture might help you experience God's presence in this prayer? For example, if you're praying for a friend who's lost a job, maybe kneeling will remind you of God's greatness when circumstances seem overwhelming. Or if you're praying for a family member who is ill, raising your hands can remind you of God our loving Father, who picks up His children when they fall. Practice your prayerful posture, and experience a conversation with God in a fresh way.

CHAPTER 9

WHEN GOD SAYS NO

Joanne knew the sound of closing doors well. She'd heard doors slamming in her face a lot lately.

Dreams of a happy marriage? Nope. *Slam!*

An exciting life in a faraway country? Nada. *Slam!*

Plans for a successful teaching career? No way. *Slam!*

OK . . . how about just a paying job? Uh-uh. *Slam!*

The word *no* echoed in nearly every area of her life.

"An exceptionally short-lived marriage had imploded, and I was jobless, a lone parent, and as poor as it is possible to be in modern Britain, without being homeless. The fears that my parents had had for me, and that I had had for myself, had both come to pass, and by every usual standard, I was the biggest failure I knew."

Joanne turned from the closed doors and found one that opened. She embraced writing. Twelve rejection notices later, Joanne (Katherine) Rowling found a publisher for *Harry Potter and the Philosopher's Stone*.

Rowling's story is fairytale-like, complete with a happy ending. But going through the "no" was painful, long, and slow. In a commencement speech at Harvard, Rowling recalls, "Now, I am not going to stand here and tell you that failure is fun. That period of my life was a dark one . . . I had no idea then how far the tunnel extended, and for a long time, any light at the end of it was a hope rather than a reality."[1]

J. K. Rowling (as far as I know) makes no claim of Christian faith—but I believe we can still learn much from her "dark tunnel" experience. Consider:

Are you or someone you know in the middle of a "dark tunnel" time right now?

Have you been knocking on the door, asking God . . . only to hear a quiet *no*?

While we crave a happy ending like Joanne's, life doesn't always work that way, does it? We like it when all the ends tie up neatly, the villain gets what's coming to him, and there's a satisfying resolution to every conflict. The hero and heroine ride off into the sunset.

Roll credits.

The reality is that sometimes we *don't* get a happy ending. When we pray, sometimes God gently says no to our prayers . . . and we may never (in this earthly life) understand why. The door we've been knocking on remains firmly closed.

The baby you've prayed for *isn't* healthy.

The adoption *doesn't* go through.

Your husband *doesn't* get the job.

Your loved one *isn't* healed.

When a friend or loved one is experiencing God's "no," it's hard to know what to do or say. We may not even know how to pray. Praying someone through the "no" is one of the most precious, intimate things a friend can do, simply because it's so hard. Our overwhelming love and compassion are dwarfed by a mountain of impossible questions. Were our requests *really* out of God's plan? How can this be wrong? What possible good could come out of such loss, rejection, pain, and disappointment? Were all those prayers in vain? What now?

We can't always know *why* God closes a door, but we *can* have the reassurance that He's the same loving, generous God who's said yes over and over.

Paul reveals his own struggle and response to God's no in his letter to the Corinthian church. After writing about a wondrous vision he had in paradise, Paul's spirits fall as he tells about a chronic earthly suffering.

> So to keep me from becoming proud, I was given a thorn in my flesh, a messenger from Satan to torment me and keep me from becoming proud. Three different times I begged the Lord to take it away. Each time he said, "My grace is all you need. My power works best in weakness." (2 Corinthians 12:7–9)

Scholars have speculated any number of things Paul's thorn might have been—physical, psychological, spiritual. We can't be certain of anything except that it caused him tremendous pain in some way, for he repeatedly implored God to remove it. Yet God's response is key:

I am enough for you.

I'm here.

My power is still intact.

As our loved ones experience God's no, we can pray that God's grace is enough for them. Rather than begging God to open doors, might we ask God to reveal His power through their weakness instead?

King David understood the brutal reality of God saying no. After David's scandalous affair with Bathsheba and the death of her husband Uriah (due to David's orchestration), David took Bathsheba as his wife and they had a son. But the child became gravely ill. Any parent can relate to the helpless, desperate feeling of watching your child suffer. Though a king, David was no different than you or me in that matter.

> David prayed desperately to God for the little boy. He fasted, wouldn't go out, and slept on the floor. (2 Samuel 12:16)

Maybe you've been there, sleeping at your child's bedside, whispering prayers throughout the night, watching for any change that might bring hope.

David didn't get the answer he so desperately prayed for.

The child died.

Given the passion with which he sought God's favor, we may be surprised at David's response to the news. His servants certainly were!

> David got up from the floor, washed his face and combed his hair, put on a fresh change

of clothes, then went into the sanctuary and worshiped. Then he came home and asked for something to eat. They set it before him and he ate.

His servants asked him, "What's going on with you? While the child was alive you fasted and wept and stayed up all night. Now that he's dead, you get up and eat."

"While the child was alive," he said, "I fasted and wept, thinking God might have mercy on me and the child would live. But now that he's dead, why fast? Can I bring him back now? I can go to him, but he can't come to me." (2 Samuel 12:20–23)

David's response may seem cold and heartless. Didn't he care that his son died? Yet a closer look shows a man so dependent upon God, so trusting in God's plan, that he worships! He willingly accepts God's awful no and chooses to look forward.

Friend, I'm not saying we should tell our loved ones to "suck it up" or "move on" when hardship hits. Yet we *can* pray that God gives them the strength and open eyes to see the doors God *is* opening. When God says no to one thing, He's saying yes to something else . . . even if that something else isn't what we currently desire.

As cancer conquered my sister's body, it became clear that God was saying no to our prayers for her healing. At some point, we all knew that our world would soon be a less beautiful, less bright and joyful place. While that didn't stop me from praying for a miracle, it shifted my focus. Rather than looking for a *result*, I began desperately looking for *God*. In the face of unspeakable loss, I needed my heavenly Father more than ever. And when we look for God, He doesn't disappoint. In the midst of that heartbreaking no, I saw God's gentle love through nurses who treated Amy with tenderness. I witnessed God's lavish generosity through friends who provided for our family. I experienced God's kindness through strangers who prayed for me at the gym or the grocery store. My dad, who slept on a cot next to his dying daughter through her last days, calls that year of desperation "the most profound year" of his life. Not the most painful. Not the most bitter. Not the most gut-wrenching.

Profound.

I actually looked up "profound" to be sure he and I were on the same page. It means "going far beneath what is superficial, external, or obvious; having deep insight or understanding; pervasive or intense."[2]

My elderly father—a deeply Christian man in his eighties, a retired seminary professor, a former pastor, and a popular Christian author—experienced God in a deeper, more intense way than he *ever* had. Through God's "no," my dad turned to God . . . and found anew his loving Father with outstretched arms and a tender love.

Psalm 56:8 paints a beautiful picture of God's compassion toward us in the midst of the heartache of God's no:

> You keep track of all my sorrows. You have collected all my tears in your bottle. You have recorded each one in your book.

Praying our loved ones through God's "no" gives us the opportunity to *be* God's strength in their weakness, to demonstrate His tender heart, and to stand with them as they search for the next open door. It's not about having "the right words." It might just be having His words and a listening ear.

PRAY TODAY

Take a puzzle piece and tape it inside your Bible. Use it as a reminder that we only get to see a *part* of the bigger picture God is creating. When you struggle with a no, look at the puzzle piece and ask God to give you His peace, and to help you trust His good plans. Perhaps your no is someone else's yes. Or perhaps God is guiding you to an open door that only He can see.

CHAPTER 10

WRITING YOUR NAME ON THE WALL

The Rescuer's Wall holds thousands of names. And the database of rescue stories received by Yad Vashem (an organization that honors Holocaust Rescuers) is vast. Each name is a tribute to a courageous soul, a name that will forever be engraved on someone's life. Every name is linked to a life, or thousands of lives, changed forever.

Whose names are on *your* wall?

Who has made a mark on *your* life by carrying your heartaches to the feet of Jesus?

Pause here and reflect. Say each name out loud.

Some of us will speak many names—it's certainly taken a small army to shoulder the burdens you've endured.

Maybe you only uttered the names of a few close friends who shared your darkest days.

And it's possible that you stayed silent, wondering "Who *has* prayed me through these challenges?" In this earthly life, you may never know of that Sunday school teacher or neighbor who whispered precious prayers into God's ear on your behalf.

It's good to realize we're not in this alone, isn't it? A "verbal memorial" like the one you just created gives hope, filling our hearts with joy and gratitude.

Now, think about this:

Whose wall could your name be on?

Take time to think through the names of people you've prayed through a difficulty. Whose name have you spoken to God again and again and again? You know those prayers . . . the ones where you imagine God sighing and saying, "You want to talk about her *again?*" (Of course, God wouldn't say that! But we sometimes think He gets tired of hearing us bring up the same issues, don't we?)

It's likely you mentioned close friends and family members. Or you spoke the name of someone in a small group Bible study. You may have lifted up the name of someone you've never even met face to face! There are countless "walls" out there in desperate need of names. Many Holocaust rescuers didn't stop at helping those in their communities—some crossed oceans and went to different countries to help the most vulnerable.

Are you willing to do the same through prayer? Interceding for someone may mean crossing religious or political oceans. After all, Scripture exhorts us to pray for our leaders:

> I urge you, first of all, to pray for all people. Ask God to help them; intercede on their behalf, and give thanks for them. Pray this way for kings and all who are in authority so that we can live peaceful and quiet lives marked by godliness and dignity. (1 Timothy 2:1–2)

If you think *you've* got an issue with a community or political leader, the early Christians had even more reason to resist this command. Franklin Graham gives a fascinating bit of context to the passage.

> Understand that the Apostle Paul is writing this instruction to his protégé Timothy at a time when the vile emperor Nero was at the helm of the vast Roman Empire. Christians

were viciously persecuted, clothed in wild animal skins and put in the arena before hungry lions, even covered red in pitch and used as human lanterns to light the streets of Rome. Nevertheless, the aged apostle, who would soon be martyred during Nero's reign of terror, instructs Timothy to make prayer for the rulers of his day—including the deranged Nero—a personal priority.[1]

Can you commit to coming alongside your political leaders, lifting their name up before Jesus? What might happen in our world if you shared their burdens in prayer? What might happen in their hearts . . . and in yours?

Paul also repeatedly asked people to pray for him and other apostles in ministry:

Dear brothers and sisters, I urge you in the name of our Lord Jesus Christ to join in my struggle by praying to God for me. Do this because of your love for me, given to you by the Holy Spirit. (Romans 15:30)

If we're honest, sometimes praying for our church leaders can be hard. Churches frequently become a bit like family, complete with competition, disagreements, and grudges. I'd challenge you to set aside those differences and come alongside your church leaders in prayer. Rather than a generic "Lord, help Pastor Greg," take the time to personally (and persistently) ask your leaders how you can pray for them.

If your prayer plate isn't full, remember that Peter and John also demonstrated the importance of praying for new Christians: "As soon as they arrived, they prayed for these new believers to receive the Holy Spirit" (Acts 8:15).

Beginning a life of faith can be a complete 180-degree shift for many people. The Bible seems big and confusing. There might be terminology or "Christian-ese" that doesn't make sense. Everyone else seems to know what to do . . . am *I* doing it right? In Luke 8, Jesus shares the parable of the sower and the seeds, reminding us of the countless distractions and pitfalls that can hinder God's love from truly taking root in a heart. New Christians need prayer support. They need someone who will commit to lifting up their journey, and praying with them through life's challenges.

Every summer, countless churches hold vacation Bible programs. While these weeklong events are full of games, snacks, and fun, they're also a powerhouse of spiritual faith formation. Thousands of children make a faith decision, starting their journey as a follower and friend of Jesus. If your church's VBS leader gave you the first name of *one* child who made a commitment to Christ, would you pray for that child throughout the year? How might God use your prayers to nurture the heart of a child?

Looking for more walls to write your name on? Scripture also commands us to pray for Christians around the globe.

> Pray in the Spirit at all times and on every occasion. Stay alert and be persistent in your prayers for all believers everywhere. (Ephesians 6:18)

If you ever have the opportunity to experience worship in another country, jump on it! There's something awe-inspiring to realize that people all over the planet worship God. I've been blessed to worship with Christians in India, Thailand, Norway, Scotland, the Dominican Republic, Costa Rica, and Zambia. Hearing familiar praise songs in another language gives a glimpse of what heaven might be like. Meeting Christian brothers and sisters who share the same worries, heartaches, and distresses reminds us that *everyone* needs Jesus.

Why not make global prayer a part of your everyday practice? To make it meaningful, connect with a missions group online, or better yet, have coffee with a missionary the next time he or she visits your church. Ask specifically how you can pray for the people in that community. Your consistent, thoughtful prayer can bring comfort and hope to Christians you might never meet in this life.

As a follower of Jesus, you're fully equipped to pray with power right now.

You don't have to take a six-week class at your church in order to achieve "Effective Pray-er" status. God doesn't *only* listen to Christians of a certain age. You don't need a seminary degree that gives you the right words to say. It's not mandatory that you've memorized countless Bible passages. God designed you in His image, giving you His traits of tenderness and compassion. Through Jesus, He's granted you a relationship with Him, calling you His friend (Romans 5:11). As you sit here reading this page, you've got everything you require to pray and change the lives of people around you.

Exciting, isn't it?

Here's a truth you may never have considered: *God doesn't need us to do His miracles for Him.*

Of course our prayers matter! Jesus valued and even modeled prayer. But consider the fact that God is 100 percent capable of healing, restoring, bringing peace and resolution whether or not we ask Him.

So why bother? What difference does it make? Why is prayer such a big deal?

Instead of looking at prayer as your obligation, look at it as an opportunity. Rather than an inconvenience, consider it an invitation. God welcomes you into the process of change. He allows *you* to play a part in the unbelievable, jaw-dropping plans He's revealing. The Creator grants *you* a part in His masterpiece. Jesus crooks His finger, beckoning you to be "in on" something surprising.

Prayer is a privilege.

The Holocaust rescuers sacrificed much to bring hope and life. Some gave the ultimate sacrifice. What does prayer cost you? You'll spend time on your knees before God. Carrying someone's heartaches may cost a few tears. Crying out to God requires an emotional investment. Immersing yourself in someone's pain is a lavish gift to them.

Give generously. God gave *you* the precious gift of relationship and communication with Him. Your voice, your heart, your passionate pleas . . . those are powerful, friend. Use that voice, heart, and passion to empower the powerless.

Become part of someone's story.

Open the door, invite someone in.

Write your name on the wall.

PRAY TODAY

Sit down with a wall calendar and your contacts list. Put one name from your contacts list (or your address book) on each weekday date of the calendar. On the weekends, write the name of a political leader and a church leader. When you reach the end of your list of contacts, start over again. Continue through the entire year. Then commit to praying for each of these people on their "day." Listen for what God might tell you they need to hear. Pray a Scripture over that person if you're not sure what to pray. Call, email, or text the person if God gives you a message, or if you want to pray with them personally.

CONCLUSION

W ill you pray for me?"

You and I hear those words every week, whether it's a plea on social media, a phone call, a conversation, or a text. We need Jesus, and we need people to help us carry our heartaches to Him. The load is just too great to bear alone.

Yet, if we're honest, sometimes prayer can become rote. There are times when it feels like mere words, or worse, a laundry list of "God, please . . ." We bow our heads at breakfast, lunch, and dinner—set times with set prayers. We join hands and pray before bed, but words and heart just aren't meshing. Maybe your heart is overwhelmed at the hardships around you. Maybe you're floundering to keep your own head above water. Maybe you're distracted. Maybe you've become hopeless. Maybe it's simply been a long time since you've seen or experienced God.

It's my prayer for *you* that, as we've shared thoughts and experiences in this book, you've become excited at the idea of praying. I'm so grateful that you chose to spend time with me in the pages here—thank you for reading this book. I hope that some spark has ignited that "wow" in your spirit—that prayer *can* be something amazing and powerful and exciting again. I pray that your conversations with God become fervent and even animated!

But be prepared, friend.

Prayer changes you. How could it *not*?

Prayer gives us access into a holy space. It immerses us in His presence, bathing us in God's attention. Prayer nurtures our relationship with our Savior. Jesus described it this way:

> Yes, I am the vine; you are the branches. Those who remain in me, and I in them, will produce much fruit. For apart from me you can do nothing. (John 15:5)

A vine and its branches are one cohesive organism, functioning together and working toward a common goal. To get a picture of what Jesus meant, reflect back to the last time you saw a lush tomato plant, heavy with bright red fruit. Or maybe your mouth starts watering at a tree laden with apples. In its fruit-bearing stage, the plant completely transforms—it looks different, smells different, feels different, and even takes on a different purpose. A fruitful tree gives life and nourishment!

Purposefully, passionately interceding for our loved ones requires that we spend time in God's presence, firmly fixing our branches to His vine. Interceding means bearing someone's burden, laying that heartache before Jesus, and listening for His response. That intentional, sacrificial act of remaining in Christ on behalf of someone else transforms us. We can't help but change when we spend time soaking in God's presence, seeking His provision. Attached to the vine, fruit-bearing branches change from blossom to bud to fruit. Perhaps that's why Paul exhorted the Christians in Thessalonica to "Never stop praying" (1 Thessalonians 5:17). He knew that a constant, abiding relationship with God would sustain the new believers, ultimately changing them from the inside out.

As you pray for others, God will change your *vision*—the way you see people, the way you view

God, the way you perceive problems and even words. And time with God can even change your *visage* or appearance.

Moses had a unique relationship with God. Exodus 33:11 tells us, "Inside the Tent of Meeting, the LORD would speak to Moses face to face, as one speaks to a friend."

What does your face look like after spending time with your favorite friend? What does your body language communicate? Chances are, you come into the room with energy and a smile. You talk exuberantly, telling a funny story your friend shared. You're energized and joyful. The same can be true when you spend time with Jesus.

Jump back to Moses and his talks with God. While Moses didn't actually *see* God's face (Exodus 33:23), it's clear that he had an intimacy with the Lord. After spending time with God, Moses *looked* different! As the leader came down from Mount Sinai, where he'd spoken with God for forty days, the Israelites got an eyeful.

"Pssst, um . . . do you see what I see?" a man whispers to his neighbor.

"What's up with Moses's face," hisses a wife to her husband, digging her elbow in his ribs.

A small boy points (as kids like to do), calling out loudly, "Look, mommy! Moses is *glowing!*"

(Of course followed by a hurried "shush" from his mother. "It's not polite to point!")

Moses wasn't even aware that his face had a radiance to it. He actually glowed from the glory of God's presence! People could see the change in him, and it was so shocking to them, he covered his face with a veil (Exodus 34:29–35).

Have you ever encountered someone who exudes the joy of the Lord? They may not actually glow, but you can almost *see* God's joy radiating from their countenance. Or perhaps you've met someone who seems to wear God's peace like a comfortable wrap. Maybe you've had a conversation with someone, and walked away with a sense that God's wisdom rested on her in an almost tangible way. Communion with Christ can change you in ways you never imagined!

I prayed to the LORD, and he answered me. He freed me from all my fears. Those who look to him for help will be radiant with joy. (Psalm 34:4–5)

So all of us who have had that veil removed can see and reflect the glory of the Lord. And the Lord—who is the Spirit—makes us more and more like him as we are changed into his glorious image. (2 Corinthians 3:18)

Spending time with God—even when we're bearing a friend's hardship—can leave us radiant. (Now there's a facial I'll bet your local spa doesn't offer. Maybe they should!) That's an exciting change! As you intercede for loved ones, you have the privilege of reflecting the glory of the Lord, shining His light into lives that are dark and desolate. And as *their* hearts are brightened, *your* entire being may be lightened.

Embrace the power and beauty of interceding for others.

Approach God's throne joyfully and expectantly.

Bring enthusiasm back to the privilege of prayer.

Your friend God is waiting with open ears.

NOTES

Introduction

1. Yad Vashem, "Women of Valor: Women Who Rescued Jews During the Holocaust," yadvashem.com, www.yadvashem.org/yv/en/exhibitions/righteous-women/eck.asp (accessed August 2018).
2. Visit to United States Holocaust Memorial Museum by author, June 2018.
3. Scripture quotations marked TPT are from The Passion Translation®. Copyright © 2017, 2018 by Passion & Fire Ministries, Inc. Used by permission. All rights reserved. ThePassionTranslation.com.

Chapter 1

1. Tammy Real-McKeighan, "Former Hostage Made a Journey of Forgiveness," freemonttribune.com, https://freemonttribune.com/news/local/former-hostage-made-a-journey-of-forgiveness/article_07ff4480-f056-11e1-b017-001a4bcf887a.html (accessed August 2018).
2. Corrie Cutrer, "Forgiven to Forgive," todayschristianwoman.com, www.todayschristianwoman.com/articles/2013/august/forgiven-to-forgive.html (accessed August 2018).

Chapter 2

1. Howard Taylor and Geraldine Taylor, *Hudson Taylor in Early Years: The Growth of a Soul* (Manila, Philippines: OMF Books, 1912).
2. *The Incredibles*, directed by Brad Bird (2004; Emeryville, CA: Pixar Animation Studios, 2005).

Chapter 3

1. Jeremy Berlin, "133 Years Later, Gaudi's Cathedral Nears Completion," nationalgeographic.com, https://news.nationalgeographic.com/2015/11/151105-gaudi-sagrada-familia-barcelona-final-stage-construction/ (accessed August 2018).

Chapter 4

1. Steve Rogers, interview with author, July 2018.

Chapter 5

1. P. L. Travers and Bill Walsh, writers, *Mary Poppins*, directed by Robert Stevenson (1964; Burbank, CA: Walt Disney Studios Home Entertainment, 2013), 50th Anniversary Edition Blu-ray Disc.
2. Oxford Living Dictionaries, "How Many Words Are There in the English Language?" Oxford, https://en.oxforddictionaries.com/explore/how-many-words-are-there-in-the-english-language (accessed August 2018).
3. C. S. Lewis, *Letters to Malcolm: Chiefly on Prayer*, ed. Walter Hooper (San Diego: Harcourt, Brace, Jovanovich, 1964).

Chapter 6

1. Panu Wongcha-um and Patpicha Tanakasempipat, "Throng of volunteers gather to rescue boys trapped in cave," reuters.com, www.reuters.com/article/us-thailand-accident-cave-rescuers/throng-of-volunteers-gather-to-rescue-thai-boys-trapped-in-cave-idUSKBN1JW0W7 (accessed August 2018); and Rebecca Wright and Patrick Sarnsamack, "Thai boys recall battle to survive cave ordeal—and moment they were found," CNN.com, https://edition.cnn.com/2018/07/18/asia/thailand-cave-rescue-boys-discharged-intl/index.html (accessed August 2018).
2. Dr. Travis Bradberry, "How Negativity and Complaining Literally Rot Your Brain," talentsmart.com, http://www.talentsmart.com/media/uploads/articles/pdfs/How%20Negativity%20and%20Complaining%20Literally%20Rot%20Your%20Brain.pdf (accessed August 2018).

Chapter 7

1. Joshua Levine, "Dunkirk heroes relive their memories of Operation Dynamo," dailymail.com, http://www.dailymail.co.uk/news /article-4699608/Dunkirk-heroes-tell-accounts.html (accessed August 2018).
2. Rachel Obordo, "We thought the war was lost: readers' stories of Dunkirk," theguardian.com, https://www.theguardian.com /world/2017/jul/25/we-thought-the-war-was-lost-readers-stories -of-dunkirk (accessed August 2018).
3. ABC News (Australia), "Survivors Visit Dunkirk," published on May 27, 2010, video, 2:39, https://www.youtube.com /watch?v=uDFefFho4KQ.
4. Matthew Henry, *Matthew Henry Complete Bible Commentary Online* (Thomas Nelson, 2003), www.biblestudytools.com/commentaries /matthew-henry-complete/esther/4.html.
5. Jessica van Lehn, interview with author, June 2018.

Chapter 8

1. Eric Jensen, *Teaching with the Brain in Mind*, 2nd ed., Association for Supervision and Curriculum Development, 2005, www.ascd .org/publications/books/104013/chapters/Movement-and-Learning .aspx (accessed August 2018).
2. Aaron West, "15 Worship Songs about Prayer," mediashout.com, www.mediashout.com/worship-songs-about-prayer/ (accessed August 2018).

Chapter 9

1. J. K. Rowling, "Text of J. K. Rowling's Speech," Harvard, news .harvard.edu/gazette/story/2008/06/text-of-j-k-rowling-speech (accessed August 2018).
2. "Profound," Dictionary.com, https://www.dictionary.com/browse /profound (accessed August 2018).

Chapter 10

1. Franklin Graham, "Praying for Those in Authority Is a Biblical Command," billygraham.org, https://billygraham.org/decision-magazine /october-2014/praying-for-our-leaders/ (accessed August 2018).

ABOUT THE AUTHOR

Jody Brolsma loves to pray—and as a career mom with three kids, she gets plenty of practice! She's an award-winning and best-selling author with international impact, and serves as executive editor for children and family ministry products at Group Publishing, a worldwide leader in creating Christian resources for churches. Jody's most popular books include the Pray & Play Bible series, *Men Are from Israel, Women Are from Moab*, and *Legacy of Virtue: A Devotional for Mothers*.

Help us get the word out!

Our Daily Bread Publishing exists to feed the soul with the Word of God.

If you appreciated this book, please let others know.

- Pick up another copy to give as a gift.

- Share a link to the book or mention it on social media.

- Write a review on your blog, on a bookseller's website, or at our own site (odb.org/store).

- Recommend this book for your church, book club, or small group.

Connect with us:

f @ourdailybread

⊙ @ourdailybread

🐦 @ourdailybread

Our Daily Bread Publishing
PO Box 3566
Grand Rapids, Michigan 49501 USA

✉ books@odb.org